LADYLIKE

KATE
LILLEY

LADYLIKE

UWA PUBLISHING

First published in 2012 by
UWA Publishing
Crawley, Western Australia 6009
www.uwap.uwa.edu.au

UWAP is an imprint of UWA Publishing
a division of The University of Western Australia

THE UNIVERSITY OF
WESTERN AUSTRALIA
Achieve International Excellence

National Library of Australia Cataloguing-in-Publication entry:

Lilley, Kate
Ladylike / Kate Lilley.
ISBN: 9781742584393 (pbk.)
A821.4

Cover image 'Lady' by Melissa Hardie
Typeset by Lasertype
Printed by Griffin Press

Melissa Anagrammatized (a dedication)

Misheard Aisle
Malaise Ids Her

Deliria Shames
Deliria Mashes

A Shared Simile
Harmed Liaises

Maid Airs Heels
Maid Lash Siree

Alias Mired She
Arias Shield Me

Dahlia Seem Sir
Dahlia Sires Me

Contents

Everyone knows what the female complaint is
— LAUREN BERLANT

Fifty Minutes

I recall as a child the pleasure of being at home when others were in class. In those days attendance was routine and had its rewards but by the last years of high school I was more surprised to find myself at school than out of it. I gave up wearing uniform to evade the drama of small infractions and penalties and finally stayed away altogether. In my last year I was banned from the class photo and exiled to the history classroom, tète a tète with my favourite mistress. Nothing could have pleased me more than this chance coming together of faithful attention and institutional indifference.

For a long time I didn't understand that there was something important at stake in attendance, something other than the choice between voluntarity and compulsion. The desire of students to be marked present and especially to sign a roll is in itself arresting. What I at first understood as an effect of anxiety, I came to value as more than juridical. The list of signatures on a piece of paper passed around, the piece of paper itself, memorializes a pedagogical session, the arrangement and composition of the class and the relations forged within it. Attendance represents a minima; the establishment of a *mis en scène* of possibility and impossibility, at once personal and impersonal.

In the early days of therapy when my mother was still alive, she said, 'Do you talk about me to that woman?' Of course! What else? Curator, timekeeper, treasurer. Attendance is hyperbolized and ritualized; the frame reified and magnified. Sessions are like dreams, absorbed into a rhythm of speaking silence and thinking aloud, a séance of intervals or, as Karl Abraham has it, 'successive presents', suggesting a sublime threshold, repeatedly redrawn. A galvanizing propinquity. At the end of fifty minutes, she says 'It *is* time' (her faint Scottish burr always thrills). I stand up, put my shoes back on, walk out into the light and catch whichever bus turns up. One or the other will appear – early or late or on time – and carry me away by one route or the other. Sometimes I go straight to a lecture or supervision. Another fifty minutes in which I offer myself in the guise, as Lacan has it, of 'the subject supposed to know', in a curious kind of double session. A lecturer, Pound says, in the *ABC of Reading*, is a man who must speak for an hour. If Pound had been more familiar with the etiquette of everyday teaching he would have known that, above all, the lecturer must not speak for an hour. Every second over fifty minutes sends shock waves through the room as students flee.

In grade three at South Perth Primary we were asked to bring our favourite book. I took the Oxford Matthew Arnold because Mum and Dad had been reading 'The Forsaken Merman' to me and my little sister, a lament about a mortal mother's abandonment of 'a little Mermaiden/And the gleam of her golden hair':

> Children dear, was it yesterday
> (Call yet once) that she went away?
> Once she sate with you and me,
> On a red gold throne in the heart of the sea,
> And the youngest sat on her knee.

I converted my attachment to Arnold's heartrending poem (the same poem, it turned out, left its mark on Sylvia Plath as a child) into a powerful identification with this book, and with poetry itself. Instinctively, I grasped the prophylactic possibilities of possessing a library and set out to memorize all the spines in the big bookcase in our living room, pouring over volumes filled with my mother's urgent underlinings and annotations. Side by side on the couch, one on one, I received my mother's instruction in close reading and the pathetic fallacy, *surprised by joy*.

In the criss-cross of mother and daughter, student and teacher, poetry and criticism, what is mine and what is hers? In the 1980s, in London, I wrote a chapter of my PhD thesis on *Masculine Elegy* on Wordsworth's 'Lucy' poems. From one of them, 'A slumber did my spirit seal', Mum chose her epitaph:

> No motion has she now, no force;
> She neither hears nor sees;
> Rolled round in earth's diurnal course,
> With rocks, and stones, and trees.

Now her Oxford Wordsworth is in my library and these lines, inscribed on her gravestone in Springwood, continue to speak of temporal dislocation and posthumous effects, the issue and timing of mourning. Her love and mine, our shared vocation.

The Double Session

Drafty

There's a safe house round the corner
bed's made
I have my reasons

The places of persuasion and dissuasion never end
the name of a street
the scene of a disturbance

Wide to the world
credit breached
playground blown

Rhapsody

The past is awake and stirring
in a black shirred bikini

blinding in a pyschedelic shift
like the picture of a mansion

I'll give you the benefit and take it back
like the yellow scarf I knitted and unknitted

the fleshy cactus roses
I grew the year I adored you

Sprechstimme

Beauty was never my friend.
Our birthdays were a year apart.

My roots were one foot in the amusement park
and another in a world of disappointment.

Sift and twist: twist and sift.
Chance meeting – cigarette lighter – blousy attrition.

In a nutshell success has been non-stop
since the door to the nursery closed.

I wanted to feel closer to God

I wanted to show my affection
to a beautiful Russian woman

I nominated myself
for a crash course in ejaculation

to placate my tiny pecker
you sent me a poem in friendship

you are not my kind of person
you are not what I had in mind

Collegiate

It's a buttoned-up preppy scene
with classics to make you squirm and snooze
        as they did me, in my time.

Prickle of cashmere semi-recumbent,
a scarf loosely tethered at the throat.
        How lovely you are

lounging beside Renaissance acquisitions,
whittling a bejewelled whip
        between the birth of the essay

and the death of the sonnet sequence.
What would the courtier-poets make of these
        campus cuties curled up

reading *The Emergence of Sexuality*
in a pool of fluorescent light.
        Tell me, and I mean this rhetorically,

What use is a book of women to you or me?
What hope is there for the sixteenth century,
        its manuscripts and ciphers,

its last-ditch graffiti etched on window panes
when suddenly the coffeehouses
        are bursting with pamphlets and actresses?

Pamela's reading *Shamela*
and the canon's pairing up
        with the apparatus of the modern state.

It's only a matter of time until the first campus novel lumbers into class and starts its
a) exordium b) recital c) Roman holiday

Executrice

Trance or decompensate, trick or treat,
the *Bewitched* marathon runs and runs.

Like Agnes I feel belittled,
my baroque powers of attention squandered.

Give me paper and plenty of it to curb my distraction!

If the broomstick fits so be it.
If the syllabub won't set
call it custard and none the wiser:
even prac crit tastes better with cream.

Once you start perseverating it pays to be thorough.
Henceforth languish in the rubble as one postponed.

METALAND

after Grace Crowley's 'Still Life' (1938)

Telephone, bottle, stair
before and after

not Paris
not Sydney either

the shallow secret surfaces
planes of red and green

blue and ochre
figure and ground in tandem

white smudges
returning in translation

parcelled necessaries
going here and there

Pet

The new teacher takes me out:
orchestra, revolving restaurant, lesbian bar.
I burn my leg on the exhaust of her bike.
Next time she brings a bottle of gin
and her admiration for Olivia Newton John.
Mortified, I let her do as she pleases.

When she moves in with me and my boyfriend, an alcoholic poet,
I develop a fever like *Villette* (which I haven't read yet).
It passes and the rent gets paid.
On the bus she talks about the other girls,
schools she has had to leave in a hurry.
I read their bewildered letters and disassociate.
When I stop having sex with her
she calls me a bourgeois bitch and joins a gun club.

Crush

When I say that history was my favourite
I'm thinking less of the Weimar Republic
or the militarization of Japan
than Miss R's contralto discipline
and her homemade Chanel suits.

For her I spend my afternoons
between the light blue covers
of the Cambridge History of England.
Pendant mes vacances
my special project is Eleanora Duse.

When she asks if she can keep it
I am nonchalant as hell.

Almanac

Panadol Tuesday.
The planets want me to make new commitments
but I've put my trust in ibuprofen.
You've accepted a divorce settlement: ergo, you're divorced.
Humidity – wind – pressure – boom!
Next time your father speaks to you you
better be more responsive you better lean forward.
It's the Tudor classroom making a comeback,
treason and martyrology, consanguinity and incest.
How can I teach numerology to a bunch of
chuckleheads who can't spell alms.
It's like watching Ozu after work,
seasons come and go with their log of claims,
their pre-prepared obituaries,
the same silk blouse drying on the line.
Bring out the tea cups! Put away the abacus!
It's the perfect marriage of stamina and caprice.
DNA and rooting powder following an inaudible trail
while all around us branches are preparing to speak.
In Ueno Park office parties spread out under the trees
to await the first cherry blossoms.
A child conceived tonight will be blessed
with patience for checking facts,
she will steal hearts and keep them for a while,
she will grow old and bide her time.

Human Scale

Preposterous recall (stop naming names)

Consent has many faces facets

Eidetic:

Mesmerized:

Recant and prosper if possible

Sworn

Turned out crook (as predicted)

Laughable sick feel
quite the robot

You, the undersigned (You, understood)

Talk fleecy
take me down

Mention me to me and I'll bite your head off

Tell the Truth

Tough-on-crime hindsight
studies personality the long way
including emotional and physical

Neither pleas nor threats had any effect
a libretto on the rebound sad and real
different jurisdictions same offender

Like his neighbours at the breakfast-bar
castration does not stop
regains [ ] composure

My Bad

In the doghouse my date barks back
bite-size annihilation

Behind the door the facts
the jokes of one awaiting trial

Am I under administration
or beginning to free associate?

Enter the poltergeist girls
with the hands of stenographers

Burning glances at smoko
moaning after lights out

Bookworm

I am a man of routine
she should have been at school by then
a girl like that with perfect attendance
a good reader   now she's gone
We didn't always get along . . . who does?
I was in the remainders   I didn't notice
there are chairs   noone bothers you
we were there a lot

I told her to pick out something
for herself   that was the last
I've cooperated   noone can say I haven't
pictures of my hands
the polygraph 8 times
Sweetie I'll give you a cheque before I leave

Baghdad Grammys

Prince and Beyoncé tearing up *Purple Rain*
the White Stripes thrashing like the Carpenters
returned from a sojourn in hell

Where is the Love
We are the Funk
This House is not a Home

Faith Hill comes out to say goodnight
a Pan Am hostess circa 1969
Hurry back to Nashville, Girlfriend

The guide for foreign scholars tells me
elation leads to disappointment
If supermarkets confuse you close your eyes

Forget about the food groups
once a sodomite always a sodomite

Anniversary (Summer Vacation)

Our first date was *Summer Vacation: 1999*
(*Nen no natsu yasumi*, 1988)
at the Walker St in North Sydney in 1990.
I had never been to a cinema (or anything else)
across the bridge. The film was avant-garde:
it was unclear whether the actors were girls or boys.
(They were girls playing boys. A good omen.)
We caught the train back to Town Hall station,
walked up Oxford St in the rain
and had Thai at the Silver Spoon off Taylor Square.
It no longer exists, nor does the Walker St.
All the repertory cinemas are gone:
Valhalla, Dave's Encore, the Rose Bay Wintergarden
where I first saw *Virgin Spring*.
On our second date I fell down the steps
of the Museum of Contemporary Art
and got up unshaken. (Another sign.)
The first gift I gave you was a tartan shopping trolley.
You wheeled it up and down the hall with a big grin.
You gave me your umbrella.
Since then we've lived in the top half
of a terrace in Annandale,
a crumbling georgian
beside a brothel in Darlinghurst,
an Arts and Crafts jewel box in Kings Cross
named for an ocean liner
and a warehouse in Surry Hills,
ex-hat factory and lock-up.
Clover's Harmony Park across the road
is a toy dog scene at twilight.
(You were a cat lover without a cat
until Vanessa rescued Dora.)

At the Hotel Hollywood, diagonally opposite,
aka the Nevada until 1940
when Paramount Pictures opened on Brisbane St,
Kelly McGillis played Diana Maitland,
the lesbian Professor in *The Monkey's Mask*
(aka *Poetry, Sex* in Japan)
a decade after Kathryn Murphy,
the vacillating lawyer in *The Accused*,
a decade before coming out (after Jodie),
boarding a cruise in Florida in 2009.

1-800-DENIED

Take this watch in token of my etc.
Glycerin pardon, barometric rage.
Now the dust jacket bears your name you have to wear it.

The sky's a huge screen flickering omens.
The doors and windows reek of yesteryear
and tenderness continues in every detail.

Lonely all the time until you paged me.
Cardiac personae, heavy turncoat.
Ransack a chorine's affection at your peril.

Abscond into criminal conversation.
Objection: asked and answered.
When the snow melts I'll open a candy concession

and moonlight as an accident attorney.
Gynaecologists rusticate in petite laneway luxury.
I await the southerly buster like any denizen.

Magnolia Thoughts

A garage in the Valley.

She could open the door and drive away
or drift into unconsciousness
before the ambulance.

You don't know me, you don't know my life.

That's a scene set in a pharmacy,
not a pretext for a singalong
so shut the fuck up.

I'm telling you now

don't have anything to do with fathers
or tv shows or fathers on tv shows
unless you're going to crank up the soundtrack

loud enough to attract a passing cop.

The auteur's desire for friends is touching
and I know we would get along
but sadly that will never happen.

The ensemble is cast, the map is drawn:

everything's eponymous.
Repetition of non-diegetic elements
leads to convulsions in nature

alluding to the death drive (incest).

Weather passes, prescriptions are filled,
a flower becomes a street.
What can I do?

This is Los Angeles:
I love you my darling.

The Double Session

Consider the problem of VIPs and their
need to avoid attention. I'd rather you didn't.
For the lingering pitfalls of shallow content
try out-of-town openings and location scouting
or get yourself a bankable hobby:
a humble half-timber fixer-upper
built for an aging child-star.
You can drive all over town in search of
Hollywoodiana: a model galleon
like the one on Errol Flynn's mantle
or chinoiserie and chintz, name your poison.
Where does a woman's sympathy end
and her indiscretion begin?

Mimesis can be your friend if you'll only let it.
My problem is secondary process,
how to swap psychotic transference for another city.
I'd cry my eyes out in a movie palace
every day if I could find the time
but insurance rarely reimburses labile affect.
I'll nod and then you can pick up
where you left off last time:
what the woman said to you,
how it made you feel small and want to leave,
searching for the lift and then the bus-stop,
the distant clack of typewriters in the night.
Once our work is done these tapes will be yours.

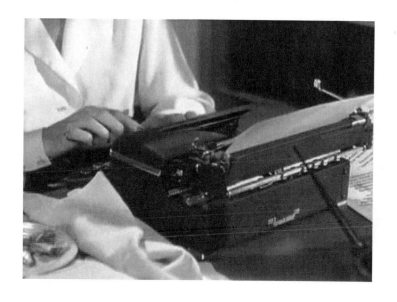

Cleft

The world is strangely changed since thou art gone.
— JONATHAN RICHARDSON JAN. 18,1726

She shall be mine, and I will make
A lady of mine own.
— WORDSWORTH

Genie

Anachronic from first to last
what's left to confess?

Tatterdemalion estate
waste and wild

I'm bound to it as if it were you
your disinhibition

Eat my words to keep them
from resembling your loose lips

This scatterbrained year read roses
wattle for laurel

Names pass you by
too far gone

Like a seance in the woods
bruises bloom

You are living on nothing but air
and out of wishes

Dress Circle

Melodramas are made for mothers.
The daughter thinks that one day
she'll graduate and take the lead.
Your right hand, little amanuensis,
eyeing off the competition.
Because I kept your secrets
I thought you were mine to keep.
Now I'm off the hook and at a loss.
Tra la la la la triangle
what'll I do without you?

When Ladies Meet

Goodbye Mama, you made me what I am
Impeccable, light-fingered little Marnie/Margaret/Peggy
You can keep the mink I stole for you
I'm young and if I go now I won't have to lose my mind
That ship at the end of the street is my ticket out and I mean
    to take it
I'll wake up in Buenos Aires, my yellow handbag bobbing
    through the crowd
I'll find Mildred at the perfume counter of a *grand magasin*
She'll show me the ropes and there'll be nothing untoward
    (I'm no Veda)
We'll work side by side and put everything into the business
A mother and daughter salon in a swanky part of town
She'll do front of house, I'll keep the books
We'll laugh and fix each other's hair and never look at a man
We'll be good together

Miltonic

Press hash and state your business somewhat loudly
while organic intermediates clear a path

what turns up's somewhat lucid ceaseless
an expurgated text unfit for work

mourning's hard to metabolize
the party's themeless don't even come

sweep the strings and hold for pastures new
woeful shepherdess

(metaphor) (condensation)
acid mantle blue

LITTLE Maisie

poor LITTLE monkey deep LITTLE cup LITTLE
unspotted soul LITTLE mutilated world inexhaustible
LITTLE stream queer LITTLE laugh LITTLE bewildered
ears LITTLE home LITTLE duenna LITTLE pamphlets
LITTLE gasp LITTLE lodging LITTLE looks LITTLE
glimpses LITTLE wonder LITTLE laugh a LITTLE
wider LITTLE crooked LITTLE mite LITTLE book
LITTLE booby smart LITTLE girl tight LITTLE plug
horrid LITTLE charge LITTLE nuisance LITTLE triangle
LITTLE clasp LITTLE waif LITTLE chimney LITTLE
fire LITTLE feathered

Maisily

confusingly immensely peculiarly soothingly brightly gravely
fortunately dazzlingly strikingly soundlessly splendidly
faintly sighingly privately repeatedly roundly educationally
confidentially honourably lightly uncontrollably absently
vaguely painfully perpetually violently impartially tenderly
beautifully remotely scarcely exactly particularly absolutely
comfortably extraordinarily deeply excessively tragically
seriously sharply necessarily precisely usually forcibly
effectually freely ominously endearingly inconsequently
temporarily intensely scarcely absolutely quietly insidiously
directly promptly clearly ingenuously speciously superbly
wholly eagerly irrepressibly direly sharply unexpectedly
utterly hideously oddly evidently tremendously infallibly
resignedly entrancingly thoughtfully lucidly merrily sensibly
fondly charmingly lucidly slowly cordially passionately
literally handsomely gravely naturally heroically sincerely
dimly devoutly fatally lately immensely interestedly
domestically accidentally accordingly unexpectedly
subsequently habitually informally submissively candidly
resolutely perceptibly mutely gallantly speedily cheerfully
excitedly delightfully quietly hilariously queerly composedly
circuitously uncommonly instantly marvellously
conscientiously abruptly notoriously superlatively nervously
curtly doggedly conspicuously disgustingly formerly
wistfully abominably blessedly profusely breathlessly
previously exultantly dolorously discernibly remonstrantly
strangely advantageously ineffaceably gleefully touchingly
pressingly musingly obscurely gracefully adequately
airily ideally gawkily confusedly logically provisionally
prohibitively ultimately irrevocably supremely luckily
exactly hastily excessively crazily criminally majestically sadly
singly gradually inscrutably thriftily serenely undeniably

proportionately markedly firmly plainly inaudibly fancifully
bravely interestedly unspeakably audaciously basely
freshly half-heartedly insidiously appallingly breathlessly
crudely disconnectedly presently impartially rejoicingly
explicitly indecently incongruously incontestably sturdily
completely rigidly desolately resentfully sightlessly blankly
simultaneously brokenly judiciously separately wistfully
stupidly actively lamely feebly decently rapidly distressfully
indignantly deludedly wildly exuberantly

Seal

Somewhere in Melbourne
your headstone
brother before us

You left him
he came back
to die

To say goodbye
to you and your new
baby boy

Abortion and then
another
home free

Minus one plus one
late life
linen

To be born
in a caul
is lucky

Coil

A lilac sheath to cover you
your wardrobe of opening nights
reduced to a simple party dress
snipped curls in plain paper
your bed hacked to pieces for the skip

Lily-leaf
weeping willow

You go on living
happen never happened

Ladylike

Behold my innocence after such disgrace
Dares show an honest and a noble Face
Hence forth there needs no mark of me be kn
For the right Counterfeit is herein shown

Ætatis meæ proxemo 22° Ianuar stilo novo vicesimo primo 1663 :

Ladylike

I rode to Hide-Park in open view
of that celebrious cavalcade

A may-game to the town
a punctual lie
befitting a person of quality

In Durham Yard
embellished & adorned
I cheated you & you me

You a Lord
& I a Princess

Manors, leases, parks & the like rhapsodies

I was promised a sky colour'd petticoat
& a podsway gown

new holland for smocks
& all things necessary

To deceive the deceiver is no deceit

Trimmed also with scarlet ribbands
she (veiling her face with her fan)
laughed at him
to the great observation of the court

A notorious notable person in these festivous times
my fortune frowardly shrunk into nothing
I would have entered any other house
had I found the doors open

Pity my ruines
these novels of my life
unsufferable mischiefs have at last exorted from me

It hath been my mishap to miscarry
an affair in the English tongue
(locked repository of excellencies)

Though envious clouds obscure my brightness
there is nothing of lewdness, baseness or meanness
in the carriage of this noised story

I am --ladies -- your devoted handmaid

Ane suit of podasey

Podesway
Padua say
Pou-de-soie
Paduasoy
Poyedesey

Spanish taffetie

The Ladies Dictionary

The fairer the woman the more gillot

quatrefoil of slut's wool
catty corner to the doxy drab

strumpet of the architraves
what a dirty puzzle you are

slattern punck
logarithmical hussy

vixen
fixen
vexer

obtuse jade

Quality if rightly taken
carries with it something extraordinary

if she be rich she must be a Gentlewoman
a Tree which shrinks in its Leaves
shamefacd tho neverso lightly

A Ladies Credit is of equal bashful niceness
a small touch may wound and destroy it
ringing *Changes* on all *accidents*
making them tunable

drawing like the painful Bee
a Mass of Hony out of Flowers of various Scents

A woman hath no clergy

One woe courteth another

Artemisia countrified

Now teach me, maid composed,
To breathe some softened strain
> — COLLINS, 'ODE TO EVENING'

By the way Minx these byways are more than pleasant
stay with me until the leaves cover the ground:
O pillowtop dainty truckstop
I'll read to you from a treatise on disappointment
imperfect enjoyment doesn't faze me in fact it's a bonus
I've said what I have to say now it's up to you
(believe that and you'll believe anything)

My will sweeps the city (automatic message)
conjugal threadcount
the long life of arcades
inhaling and exhaling
streets like the back of my hand
You'll come back when you're ready
Trinket my mind's set

Heidiland

Not every day can be Interlaken

Meadows stitched with eidelweiss
a chalet built around a poem

Milkmaids line the Golden Pass
with Vanilla Plunder for the rescue team

Entablature of heirloom ramblers
gathering cuckoo clocks

Lauralude

Processed haughty coquette
footling kewpie
gingham haze

Vellum umber rubbermaid
a fair sea of permanent waves
cornflower corrigenda

The Garden of Alla

Nazimova the Unforgettable
hears the coming of sound
and opens a bungalow court
on the Strip opposite Schwab's

A gem of comfort
in a setting of romance

The swimming pool shaped like the Black Sea
is studded with stars every night

Japanese waiters pour champagne
Clara Bow swan dives
into the underwater lights
leaving a trail of silver bubbles

On Sunday afternoons the piano roll croons
Alla my heart is lonely, I want you only

Alla's girls paint leaves
dance in silhouette
Iris Tree composes a poem

At dusk the 8080 club
(what's left of it) assembles

Madame is Marguerite in a drift of camelias
Peter in navy serge
Nazimova in black silk pajamas by Rambova
(born Winifred Shaugnessy of Phoenix Az)

Fitzgerald sends a postcard to himself

Dear Scott
 I'm living in Paradise
Yours, Scott

the Pansy Craze is over
the Garden's down on its luck

from her sunny perch on the second floor
Alla watches the hummingbirds
reads Spinoza on necessity
hopes for a comeback

tenant of Villa 24
next stop Forest Lawn

Round Vienna

Fraud's Dora

A girl may harden herself
in the conviction that she does possess a penis
I had the usual feeling of anxiety that one has
in the somewhat haphazard order in which it recurs
I saw myself particularly distinctly
'Why did I say nothing about the scene by the lake
for some days after it had happened?
Why did I then suddenly tell my parents about it?'
A normal girl, I am inclined to think,
will deal with a situation of this kind by herself
I will begin by mentioning the subject-matter
he intended to come forward as a suitor one day
what was the source of the words 'if you like'?
there was a question mark after this word, thus 'like?'.

She might calmy read whatever she chose
'vorhof' ['vestibulum'; literally 'fore-court'] –
an anatomical term for a particular
region of the female genitals
She had left home and gone among strangers
to this came the addendum not the least sadly
her father's heart had broken with grief and longing
he could not get to sleep without a drink of brandy
sexual satisfaction is the best soporific
She then recognized these words as a quotation
her knowing all about such things and at the same time
pretending not to know was really too remarkable
the feelings of pity for him which she remembered
from the day before would be quite in keeping with this

In repeating the dream she said 'two hours'
so here we were back again at the scene by the lake
no sooner had she grasped the purport of his words
than she had slapped him in the face and hurried away
'you know I get nothing out of my wife'
Her father was dead and she had left home by her own choice
this fact determines the psychical coating
In the background of the picture there were *nymphs*
the neurosis had seized upon this chance event
and made use of it for an utterance of its own
They are therefore questions referring to – the genitals
wandering about in a strange town was overdetermined
my expectations were by no means disappointed
You give me a fortnight's warning just like a governess

Anisotropy

Material that has no counterpart
is evidence of love

and what else   *spoiled for another*
the first real good object

the graph is indecisive
the interpretation was not quite right

tell me what you want me to know
biter twice bitten

a dwelling place that has been destroyed
is now at your disposal

For 'melancholia with long intervals'
read 'melancholia with short intervals'

One letter at a time   a pin upon the floor
something was said about a dust-pan and brush

On being given a pencil she calls it a pen-knife
'it is what you write with'

No   it is a door-key

dull-sharp
salt-sugar
taste and charm

She says they are unalike
o with a piece cut out is e

'water-closet' was repeated with especial frequency
(acute intestinal malady)

As interesting are the menstrual melancholias
or those which are homicidal

Grievances followed in chronological order

belle indifférence
chronic affection
excess efficiency

It was a fine day   not too hot
the scene had crushed her hopes

She stood as though spellbound
a burning wish
applying criticism

'Degenerate' would distort the meaning of that word
(clacking, grimaces)

No reply

A little cocaine to untie the tongue
the procedure never fails

Since then the lady has sung in public

Sidonie

A single case not too pronounced
a misfortune like any other
a *cocotte* in the ordinary sense
a severe beauty mature but still youthful
a well-made girl intact unversed
she did not scruple to appear
in the most frequented streets
she was in fact a feminist

So complicated and hard to effect
the deeper heterosexual current
falls to the ground   into the cutting
So it turned out . . . how very interesting
nor was she so incensed
at the part played by subsequent forgetting

Marie

A private view of the royal trousseau
in the Rue de la Paix in 1907

stomacher of diamond olive leaves fit for a queen

a princess gown
pink satin and velvet with steel points

silver cluny lace
cherry tulle
mousseline de soie

Napoleonic fur toques decked with feathers

ostrich
marabou
aigrette

Narjani's *volupté*

téleclitoridiennes
mesoclitoridiennes
paraclitoridiennes

Give her an inch!

Notes

Many thanks to Lauren Berlant for permission to take my epigraph from her book, *The Female Complaint: The Unfinished Business of Sentimentality in American Culture* (Duke UP, 2008).

'Cleft' is dedicated to my mother, Dorothy Hewett (1923–2002).

'Ladylike' draws on the pamphlets associated with the notorious case of the bigamist Mary Carleton, executed in 1673, and texts contemporary with it. See my essays, 'The German Princess Revived: the Case of Mary Carleton', in *Expanding the Canon of Early Modern Women's Writing*, ed. Paul Salzman, Newcastle: Cambridge Scholars Press, 2010, 113–124, and 'These Novels of My Life': Mary Carleton's crimes', *Australian Feminist Studies*, 25, Number 65, 2010, 265–279. Both can also be found on my <academia.edu> page.

The raw materials of *Round Vienna* are texts from the early history of psychoanalysis, chiefly Freud's case studies, 'Fragment of an Analysis of a Case of Hysteria' ['Dora'], 'The Psychogenesis of a Case of Homosexuality in a Woman' [Sidonie Csillag], 'Frau Emmy von N.' and 'Miss Lucy' from *Studies on Hysteria*; Silas Weir Mitchell, *Clinical Lessons on Nervous Diseases*; the writings of Marie Bonaparte and the events of her life as reported in the press. Collaged images by Melissa Hardie. *Round Vienna* was first published as an illustrated chapbook by Vagabond Press, Sydney, 2011, with images by Melissa Hardie.

Acknowledgements

Some of these poems, sometimes in different versions, were previously published in *Jacket, Jacket2, Southerly, Black Box Manifold, The Age, The Sun-Herald, Snorkel*, NZEPC (*Home & Away 2010*), *Best Australian Poems* 2005, ed. Peter Craven, Melbourne: Black Inc, 2005, *Women's Work*, eds Eva Salzman and Amy Wack, Bangor, Wales: Seren Press, 2008, *Over There: Poems from Singapore and Australia*, eds John Kinsella and Alvin Pang, Singapore:Ethos Books, 2008, *The Best Australian Poetry 2009*, ed. Alan Wearne, St Lucia: University of Queenland Press, 2009, *The Penguin Anthology of Australian Poetry*, ed. John Kinsella, Camberwell, Vic.:Penguin, 2009, *Best Australian Poems* 2010, ed. Robert Adamson, Melbourne: Black Inc, 2010, *Best Australian Poems* 2011, ed. John Tranter, Melbourne: Black Inc, 2011. 'METALAND' was commissioned for 'Poets Paint Words 2' by the Sydney Writers Festival. 'When Ladies Meet' was commissioned by the Red Room Company, Sydney. *Round Vienna* was first published as an illustrated chapbook by Vagabond Press: Sydney, 2011. Grateful thanks to the editors of all these publications and to those who invited me to participate in readings.